HOW MACHINES WORK

AIRCRAFT

IAN GRAHAM

A330-200F AIRBUS

A^+

Smart Apple Media

Smart Apple Media is published by Black Rabbit Books
P.O. Box 3263, Mankato, Minnesota 56002

Printed in Hong Kong

Library of Congress Cataloging-in-Publication Data

Graham, Ian, 1953–
    Aircraft / Ian Graham.
    p. cm.—(Smart Apple Media. How machines work)
    Includes index.
    Summary: "Describes in detail how the engines, wings, and controls of airplanes and helicopters work"—Provided by
publisher.
    ISBN 978-1-59920-292-1
    1. Airplanes—Juvenile literature. I. Title.
TL547.G73 2009
629.133'3—dc22

2008002399

Created by Q2AMedia
Series Editor: Honor Head
Book Editor: Harriet McGregor
Senior Art Director: Ashita Murgai
Designers: Harleen Mehta, Mansi Mittal, Shilpi Sarkar
Picture Researchers: Amit Tigga, Poloumi Ghosh

All words in **bold** can be found in the Glossary on pages 30–31.

Web site information is correct at time of going to press. However, the publishers cannot
accept liability for any information or links found on third-party Web sites.

Picture credits
t=top b=bottom c=center l=left r=right m=middle
Cover Images: Main Image: Theflightcollection.com

Theflightcollection.com: 4, Colin & Linda McKie/ Shutterstock: 5t, Tim Jenner/ Shutterstock: 5b, Airbus 2006 -Abac effect –
HCSM: 6t, Rolls-royce: 6b, Airbus S.A.S 2005: 8, prism_68/ Shutterstock: 9t, Frank Ungrad/ Shutterstock: 9b,
Mlenny/ Istockphoto: 10b, Piotr Michal (PioM) Jaworski: 11, George Hall/ Corbis: 12, Berkaviation/ Dreamstime: 13t,
Hashim Pudiyapura/ Shutterstock: 13b, Adam Romanowicz/ Shutterstock: 16, Sierrarat/ Istockphoto: 17t,
bbossom/ Istockphoto: 17b, Aircraft Spruce Marketing/ 18t, Adventure_Photo/ Istockphoto: 18b, Science Photo Library: 19b,
Horizon International Images Limited/ Alamy: 20, Maxian/ Istockphoto: 21t, The Boeing Company: 22,
WoodyStock/ Alamy: 23, Paul Souders/ Corbis: 24, U.S. Air Force: 25t, 25b, The Boeing Company: 26,
U.S. Air Force: 28, 29b, Charles F McCarthy/ Shutterstock: 29t

Q2AMedia Art Bank: 7, 10m, 14, 15, 19t, 21, 27

9 8 7 6 5 4 3 2 1

CONTENTS

AIRCRAFT

Aircraft are amazing machines. The biggest aircraft can carry hundreds of passengers halfway around the world. The fastest can fly faster than a bullet.

SPEED AND HEIGHT

A modern airliner zooms along more than 32,000 ft. (10,000 m) above the ground. Passengers sit comfortably and hardly notice that it is moving at all. It is an almost perfect combination of power, shape, and advanced technology.

The Boeing 787 Dreamliner is Boeing's latest and most advanced airliner.

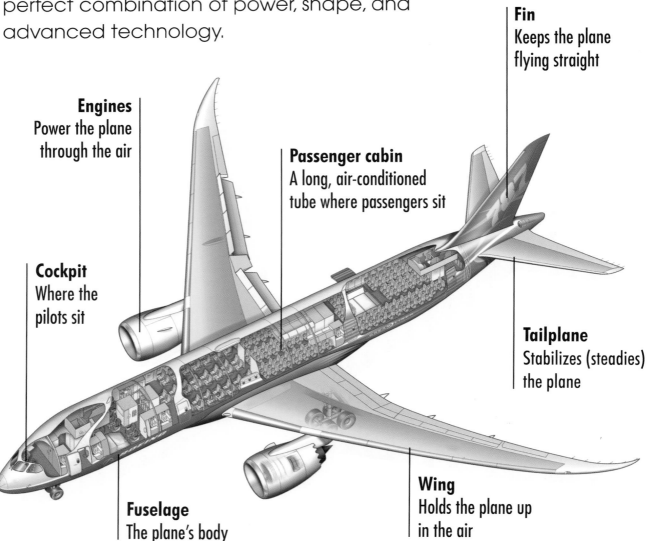

Fin
Keeps the plane flying straight

Engines
Power the plane through the air

Passenger cabin
A long, air-conditioned tube where passengers sit

Cockpit
Where the pilots sit

Tailplane
Stabilizes (steadies) the plane

Fuselage
The plane's body

Wing
Holds the plane up in the air

AIRCRAFT TYPES

There are lots of different types of aircraft. Airliners carry lots of passengers; **cargo planes** carry goods; light and ultralight planes are used for fun and transport; and business jets are used as air taxis. There are also many kinds of helicopters and military aircraft. While all of these aircraft have engines, gliders sail on air currents without any engine power at all.

DID YOU KNOW?
More than 18,000 aircraft currently fly passengers around the world.

◀ The smallest ultralight aircraft are just big enough for one person.

AIRBUS A380	
Specification	
Length:	239.5 ft. (73.0 m)
Wingspan:	261.8 ft. (79.8 m)
Height:	79.1 ft. (24.1 m)
Capacity:	850 passengers
Number of engines:	4

▼ The Airbus A380 is the world's biggest airliner. It can carry up to 850 passengers.

AIRCRAFT ENGINES

An aircraft engine's job is to provide the power to push the aircraft along the runway and up through the air. Different-sized airplanes have different types of engines.

AIRBUS A330-200F

Specification
Length: 192.9 ft. (58.8 m)
Wingspan: 197.8 ft. (60.3 m)
Height: 55.4 ft. (16.9 m)
Capacity: 76 tons (69 t) of cargo
Number of engines: 2

▼ This Airbus A330-200F has two jet engines.

▶ Rolls-Royce Trent 700 turbofan jet engine.

TYPES OF ENGINE

Small propeller planes and helicopters have piston engines. They work like car engines, but instead of turning wheels, they turn propellers or **rotor blades**. Bigger propeller planes and helicopters have **jet engines**. A jet engine that turns a propeller is called a turboprop. A jet engine that powers a helicopter is called a turboshaft. Faster planes are powered by jet engines called **turbofans**.

HOW DOES A JET ENGINE WORK?

TURBOFAN

▼ The power of a turbofan engine is provided by heating air to make it expand rapidly to produce a high-speed jet.

1. Primary air stream
Air is sucked into the center of the engine by the fan

Fan

2. Secondary air stream
Air blown around the center of the engine by the fan

3. Outer nozzle
Directs the secondary air stream backward

4. Compressor
Some of the air enters a **compressor,** which squashes it

6. Combustion chamber
Fuel burns and heats the air

5. Fuel injector
Sprays fuel into the air

7. Turbine
The hot air spins a turbine, which powers the fan and compressor

8. Hot gases thrust the plane forward

DID YOU KNOW?
Each of an airliner's jet engines is more powerful than 1,000 family cars!

TURBOPROP
A jet engine that drives a propeller

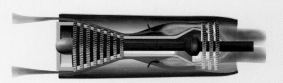

TURBOSHAFT
A jet engine that drives a shaft

WHERE'S THE ENGINE?

The engines of most airliners hang below the **wings**. This makes them easy for engineers to get to when they need to be checked or repaired. This works well for **airliners**, but not for fighter planes. Engines under a fighter's wings could be easily damaged by enemy guns and missiles. The engines on fighter planes are hidden inside the aircraft's body.

Engine nacelle
The case that holds the engine

Some jet airliners have two or four engines positioned underneath their wings.

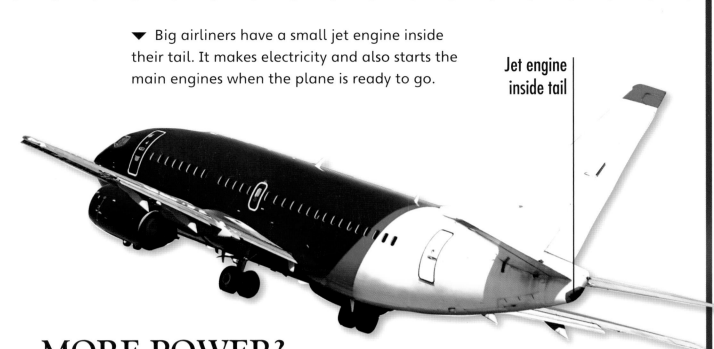

▼ Big airliners have a small jet engine inside their tail. It makes electricity and also starts the main engines when the plane is ready to go.

Jet engine inside tail

MORE POWER?

Fighter planes can produce a quick burst of extra power and speed if they need it. They might need more power to take off from a short runway or more speed to escape an enemy plane. They get the boost of power by turning on their afterburner. The afterburner sprays extra **fuel** into the hot jet coming from the engine. The fuel burns instantly and gives the plane an extra push.

Afterburner
Inside the engine exhaust nozzle

▲ Turning on an afterburner sends a jet of flames flying from a fighter's engine.

TAKING OFF

Planes can take off and fly because of the shape of their wings. Surprisingly, a plane's wings change size and shape during a flight!

WHAT WINGS DO

When a plane's wings move through air, their shape makes the air travel further over the top than underneath. This simple difference produces a force called **lift** that pushes the wings upward. Tilting the wings up at the front produces even more lift. The special shape of a wing is called an **aerofoil**. The faster an aerofoil moves, the more lift it produces.

A plane takes off when its wings lift upward more than its weight pulls downward.

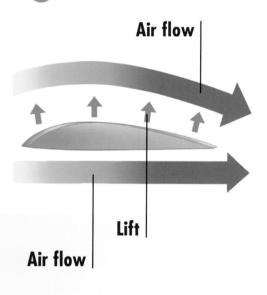

Air flow

Lift

Air flow

Wing
Made of plastic

◀ A sailplane's wings are long and thin for gliding on air currents.

DID YOU KNOW?
A glider climbs higher by hitching a ride on rising air currents.

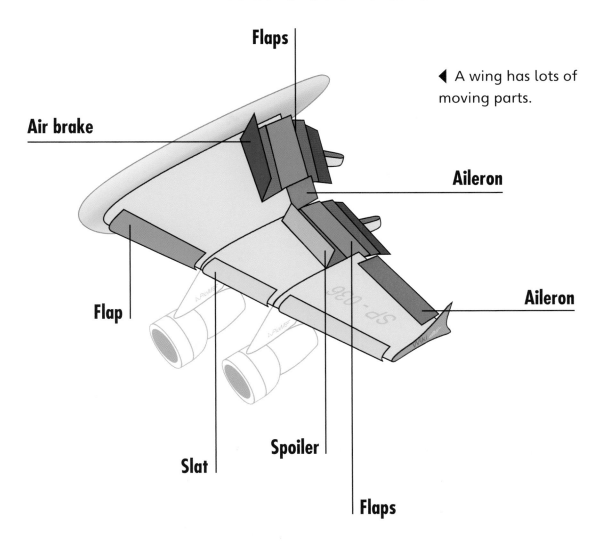

Flaps

Air brake

◀ A wing has lots of moving parts.

Aileron

Flap

Aileron

Spoiler

Slat

Flaps

THE PARTS OF A WING

An airliner's wings have moving parts that change their size and shape.

- Flaps and slats slide out from the front and back of wings. They make wings bigger and more curved so they produce more lift. They are used when a plane is flying slowly for takeoff and landing.
- Air brakes swing up on top of a wing to slow down a plane.
- Spoilers "spoil," or change, the shape of a wing and reduce the amount of lift it produces.
- Strips called ailerons tilt up or down to steer a plane.

WING STORAGE

A plane's wings have a lot of room inside. Most of the space is full of fuel because the wings are a plane's fuel tanks. There are also spaces inside the wings and body where the wheels fold away after takeoff. When the wheels are safely tucked inside, doors close over them to give the plane a smooth shape.

DID YOU KNOW?
A Jumbo Jet's wings hold enough fuel to fill the tanks of more than 3,000 cars!

Landing gear
Raised just after takeoff to make the plane more streamlined

An airliner's wheels fold up inside its wings and body just after takeoff.

▼ Some planes have turned-up wingtips called winglets to improve the airflow at the ends of the wings.

Flaps
Lowered for landing

Winglet

SPINNING WINGS

The spinning blades on top of a helicopter are long, thin wings. When they whirl around, they lift the helicopter into the air. Helicopters can hover, which means they can stay in one place in the air. This is because their spinning blades produce lift even when the helicopter itself is not moving. Most planes with wings cannot hover because their wings produce lift only when the plane is moving.

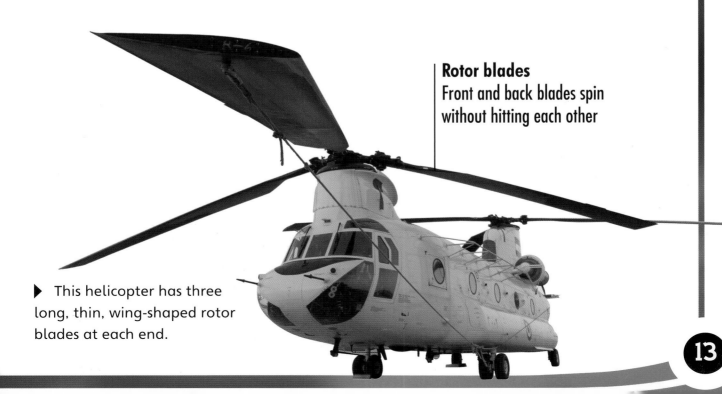

Rotor blades
Front and back blades spin without hitting each other

▶ This helicopter has three long, thin, wing-shaped rotor blades at each end.

STEERING AIRCRAFT

A pilot steers a plane by moving parts of its wings and tail. This changes the way air flows around the plane. This turns it or tips it to point in a new direction.

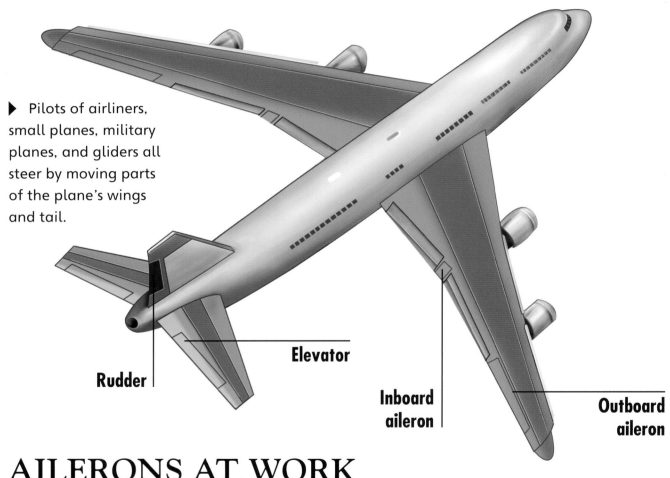

▶ Pilots of airliners, small planes, military planes, and gliders all steer by moving parts of the plane's wings and tail.

Rudder

Elevator

Inboard aileron

Outboard aileron

AILERONS AT WORK

Parts of a plane's wings and tail move to steer the plane. These parts are called control surfaces. The control surfaces in the wings are called ailerons. When the aileron in one wing tilts up, air pushes the wing down. At the same time, the aileron in the other wing tilts down and pushes that wing up. While one wing rises, the other wing falls, and then the plane turns.

PITCH, ROLL, AND YAW

A plane can be tilted or turned in three ways.

- It can tip its nose up or down. This is called **pitch**.
- It can raise one wing or the other. This is called **roll**.
- It can turn its nose to the left or right. This is called **yaw**.

Pitch is controlled by the **elevators**. Roll is controlled by the ailerons. Yaw is controlled by the **rudder**.

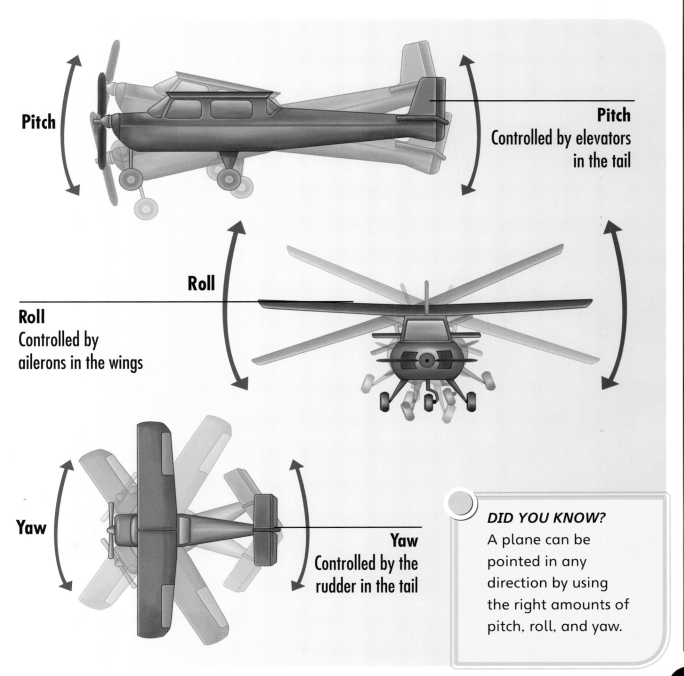

Pitch

Pitch
Controlled by elevators
in the tail

Roll

Roll
Controlled by
ailerons in the wings

Yaw

Yaw
Controlled by the
rudder in the tail

DID YOU KNOW?
A plane can be pointed in any direction by using the right amounts of pitch, roll, and yaw.

HOVER-PLANE

The Harrier jump jet is a very unusual plane. It can take off straight up in the air and hover like a helicopter. It can fly like this because it can point the jet of air from its engine straight downward. When it is hovering, the pilot tilts and turns the plane by using small jets of air from its nose, tail, or wingtips. When it flies faster, it steers in the same way as other planes.

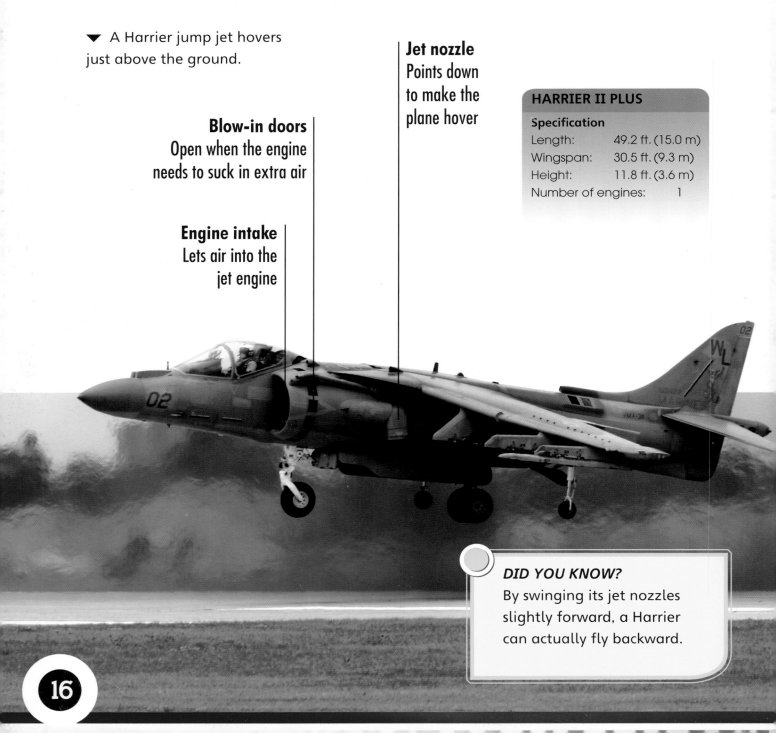

▼ A Harrier jump jet hovers just above the ground.

Jet nozzle
Points down to make the plane hover

Blow-in doors
Open when the engine needs to suck in extra air

Engine intake
Lets air into the jet engine

HARRIER II PLUS

Specification	
Length:	49.2 ft. (15.0 m)
Wingspan:	30.5 ft. (9.3 m)
Height:	11.8 ft. (3.6 m)
Number of engines:	1

DID YOU KNOW?
By swinging its jet nozzles slightly forward, a Harrier can actually fly backward.

STEERING A HELICOPTER

Helicopters are steered in a different way from airplanes. When they are flying straight, a helicopter's blades push air downward. To turn, helicopters tilt the big rotor on top. Some of the air is now pushed to one side. This blows the helicopter in the opposite direction. The tiny rotor in a helicopter's tail turns the tail. This points the helicopter in the right direction.

Main rotor

▶ Tilting a helicopter's main rotor makes the helicopter turn.

Tail rotor

BELL 407

Specification

Length:	41.7 ft. (12.7 m)
Rotor diameter:	35.1 ft. (10.7 m)
Height:	11.8 ft. (3.6 m)
Capacity:	6 passengers
Number of engines:	1

▼ A helicopter's tail rotor stops a helicopter from spinning in the opposite direction of the main rotor.

DID YOU KNOW?
The world's fastest helicopter is a Westland Lynx, which set a record of 249 mph (400 km/h) in 1986.

FINDING THE WAY

Finding your way from place to place is called navigation. Aircraft have navigation equipment to help pilots fly in the right direction.

STAYING ON COURSE

The simplest way to navigate is to use a **compass**. A compass needle always points north. Aircraft have compasses, but they usually have other ways to navigate too. Radio transmitters on the ground send out radio signals. Aircraft receive these signals so pilots can use them to fly from transmitter to transmitter.

▶ An ordinary compass needle swings too much in a moving plane. Planes need a steadier compass called a heading indicator or directional gyro, like this one.

The reading at the aircraft's nose shows the direction the plane is flying.

◀ Radio transmitters are also called beacons. Beacons send out radio signals to guide aircraft.

DID YOU KNOW?
Navigation satellites were first used to help submarines find out where they were in the ocean.

SATELLITE NAVIGATION

Many aircraft also use satellite navigation or "satnav" systems. These systems use radio signals from spacecraft to find out where the aircraft is and to make sure it stays on course.

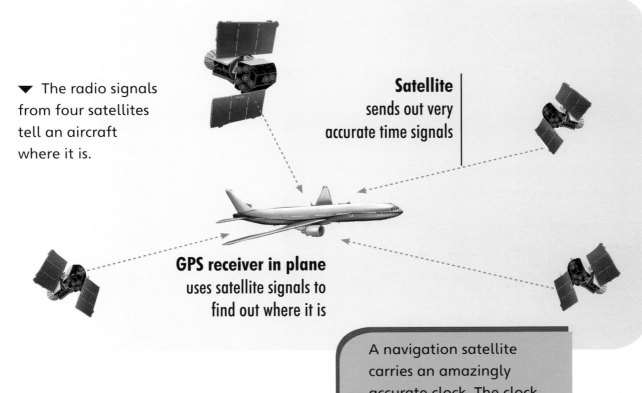

▼ The radio signals from four satellites tell an aircraft where it is.

Satellite sends out very accurate time signals

GPS receiver in plane uses satellite signals to find out where it is

SPACE STEERING

Satellites in space travel around Earth. Some of these are used for satellite navigation, or satnav. These satellites belong to the Global Positioning System (GPS). A radio receiver in an aircraft picks up radio signals from some of the satellites. It uses the signals to find out exactly how far away it is from each satellite, and then pinpoints its position.

A navigation satellite carries an amazingly accurate clock. The clock will only gain or lose one second in 300,000 years!

AIR TRAFFIC CONTROL

Pilots cannot fly wherever they want. They follow directions from air traffic controllers on the ground. This is especially important in the busy skies around airports. The controllers watch the movements of aircraft on **radar** screens and talk to the pilots by radio. The planes are guided along invisible paths in the sky that keep them a safe distance apart.

▼ An air traffic controller watches aircraft movements on a radar screen.

Screens
Show maps of the ground with the airways drawn on top

◀ This radar antenna at London's Heathrow Airport spins around, spotting planes moving around the airport.

Radar spots planes when they are too far away to see.

Radar signals
Reflected back to the antenna by the plane

RADAR

Radar uses radio waves to find aircraft. The radar antenna at air traffic control sends out radio waves in all directions. If the waves hit an aircraft, they bounce off it. Some of the waves bounce straight back to where they came from. These reflections, or echoes, make a bright spot on a radar screen that shows where the aircraft is.

Radar tower

IN THE COCKPIT

An aircraft's cockpit is its control center. It is the place where the pilots fly the aircraft. The cockpit is in the aircraft's nose.

CONTROLS

The cockpit has all the controls and instruments needed to fly an aircraft. In modern cockpits, most of the instruments have been replaced by flat-panel display screens. The screens show the crew everything they need, including the aircraft's speed, height, direction, and engine performance.

Captain's seat

Control column
Controls roll and pitch

Primary flight display

Engine display

▼ Screens in an airliner cockpit are linked to the plane's computers.

Copilot's seat

DID YOU KNOW?
A cockpit with flat panel displays is also known as a glass cockpit.

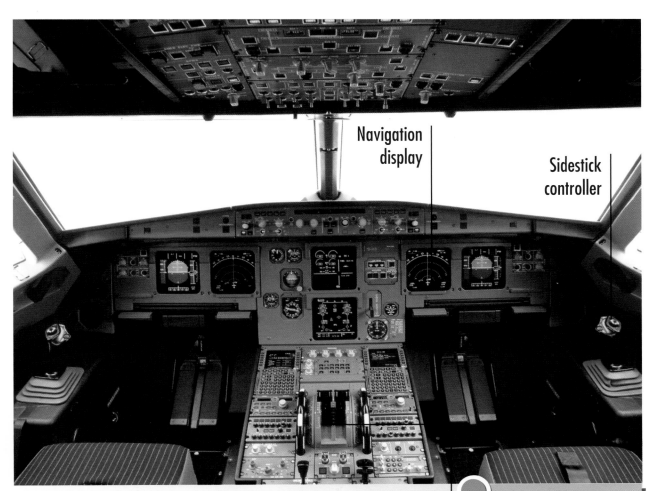

Navigation display

Sidestick controller

IN THE PILOT'S SEAT

Most planes have a control column between the pilot's knees and the rudder pedals on the floor. These are the main controls that are used to fly the plane. Moving the control column makes the plane go higher or lower or roll. Pushing the rudder pedals turns the plane's nose to the left or right. Some airliners do not have control columns. Instead, they are steered by a small hand control called a sidestick controller, found at each side of the cockpit.

The giant Airbus A380 airliner is steered by a tiny control stick no bigger than the pilot's hand.

Thrust levers
Control the power levels of the jet engines

FLYING A HELICOPTER

A helicopter has three main controls. The cyclic stick is for steering. The collective lever is moved by the pilot's left hand. Pulling it up tilts the spinning blades and produces more lift for takeoff. The rudder pedals control the small tail rotor to keep the helicopter pointing in the right direction.

A helicopter pilot's left hand controls the aircraft's height. The pilot's right hand and feet control steering and direction.

Cyclic stick
Controls steering

Collective lever
Controls height

Radio microphone
Allows pilot to talk to base

FIGHTER COCKPIT

The **cockpit** of a fighter plane is tiny and cramped. Fighter pilots often don't have time to look down at the instruments, so important information appears on a glass screen in front of them. The screen lets the pilots see the information and look at the sky at the same time.

▶ A fighter pilot looks out through the greenish glass of the cockpit head-up display.

Head-up display panel

ROCKET SEAT

If a fighter pilot has to get out of a plane in an emergency, a rocket under the seat is fired. It sends the **ejection seat** and pilot flying out of the cockpit. The pilot floats to the ground using a parachute.

Cockpit canopy
Blown clear before the pilot ejects

Pilot strapped into ejection seat

▶ A pilot from the U.S. Air Force Thunderbirds display team ejects from his cockpit during an air display.

25

AIRCRAFT DESIGN

Every aircraft is designed for a purpose. Airliners have a big body for carrying lots of passengers. Fighter planes are small, fast, and carry weapons.

BUILDING PLANES

Materials for planes have to be strong and light. A metal called **aluminum** is most commonly used. First, an aluminum frame is made. Then, thin sheets of aluminum are laid on top to make the plane's smooth shape. Some aircraft are made from lighter, stronger metals such as titanium. To save even more weight, some parts are made of plastic.

A line of Boeing 747-400 Jumbo Jets are built inside a giant aircraft construction hall.

RIB AND SPAR

The frame inside a plane's wings is like a skeleton. It is made of parts called **ribs** and **spars**. Ribs go from the front of the wing to the back. They give the wing its curved aerofoil shape. Spars are the parts that go from the plane's body to the wingtip. Spars are incredibly strong because they have to hold up the entire weight of the aircraft.

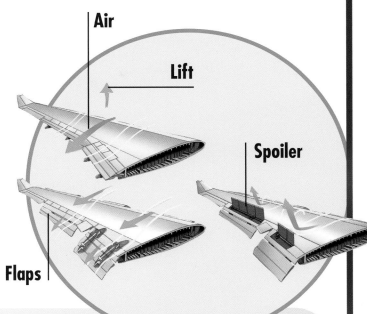

▼ The moving parts of a wing are fixed to the ribs and spars.

Air

Lift

Spoiler

Flaps

▼ Ribs and spars give wings their shape and strength.

Leading edge
The front edge of the wing

Rib
Gives the wing its shape

Spar
Runs the length of the wing

Trailing edge
The back of the wing

DID YOU KNOW?
The first plane to fly in 1903 had rib and spar wings, just like most modern planes today.

Tail fins
Angled to make the plane more stealthy

Intakes
Bring lots of air in for the plane's two powerful jet engines

SUPERSONIC

Most aircraft fly slower than the speed of sound. Sound travels through the air at about 750 mph (1,200 km/h). The fastest military planes can fly faster than sound. They are **supersonic**. Incredibly, some fighters can fly at more than three times the speed of sound. They have to be exactly the right shape to slice through the air at such a high speed. They need a sharp nose, a slim body, and thin wings.

The F-22A Raptor is a fighter designed to fly at twice the speed of sound.

DID YOU KNOW?
The speed of sound is also known as mach 1. The fastest aircraft can reach mach 3, which is three times the speed of sound.

STEALTH PLANES

Faraway aircraft in the sky are spotted by radar. The aircraft show up as bright spots moving across a radar screen. Some warplanes are specially designed so that they do not make bright dots on radar screens. Planes like this are called **stealth planes**. They are able to hide from enemy radar. It is their shape and the materials they are made from that allow them to do this. Stealth lets warplanes close in on their target without being spotted.

▼ The B-2 can travel 5,965 mi. (9,600 km) before it needs to refuel.

NORTHROP B-2 SPIRIT

Specification
Length: 68.6 ft. (20.9 m)
Wingspan: 170.9 ft. (52.1 m)
Height: 16.7 ft. (5.1 m)
Capacity: 2 (crew)
Number of engines: 4

Engines
On top to shield them from heat-seeking missiles

Weapons
Carried in two bays inside the plane's body

Wing
Made of strong plastic

Cockpit
With room for a crew of two

The B-2 Spirit bomber is a stealth plane. Its strange shape, with no body or tail, is called a flying wing.

GLOSSARY

Aerofoil Shape of a wing that produces lift

Aileron Part of a plane's wing that swivels up or down to make the plane roll

Airliner Plane designed to carry paying passengers

Aluminum Lightweight metal used to build aircraft

Cargo Goods carried by an aircraft

Cargo plane Aircraft that carries goods

Cockpit Control center of a plane, where the pilot sits

Combustion Burning

Combustion Chamber Part of a jet engine where the fuel is burned

Compass Instrument that shows directions

Compressor Part of a jet engine that squashes air inside the engine

Ejection seat Rocket-propelled pilot's seat in a fighter plane

Elevator Part of a plane's tail that swivels up or down to make the plane's nose tip up or down

Fin Part of an aircraft's tail that stands up

Fuel Substance that is burned to produce heat or power

Helicopter Aircraft that has rotor blades and is able to hover in the air

Jet engine Type of engine that works by producing a fast jet of air

Lift Upward force produced by an aircraft's wings or a helicopter's rotor blades

Navigation Setting a route and steering a plane along it

Pitch One of the three ways an aircraft can tilt or turn. When an aircraft pitches, its nose rises or falls.

Radar Method for finding aircraft by bouncing radio waves off them

Rib Part of the frame inside a wing running from front to back

Roll One way that an aircraft can turn. When an aircraft rolls, one wing rises and the other falls.

Rotor blade Long, thin wing-shaped part of a helicopter that spins

Rudder Part of an aircraft's tail fin that swivels to turn the aircraft's nose to the right or left

Spar Part of the frame inside a wing running from the plane's body to the tip of the wing

Stealth plane Plane that is hard to find by radar because of its shape and the materials it is made from

Supersonic Faster than the speed of sound

Thrust Force that pushes a plane through the air

Turbine Part of a jet engine that looks like a propeller with many blades

Turbofan Type of jet engine with a large fan at the front to suck in air

Wing Large part of a plane that produces lift when it moves through air

Winglet Small turned-up wingtip

Yaw One of the three ways an aircraft can tilt or turn. When an aircraft yaws, its nose turns to the left or right.

INDEX

Web Sites

For Kids:

http://www.azdot.gov/aviation/kids.asp

http://www.phl.org/kids_fourforces.html

For Teachers:

http://www.nasm.si.edu/wrightbrothers/classroomActivities